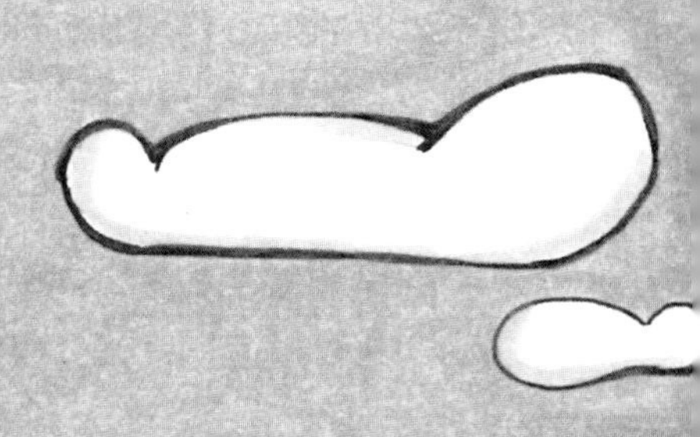

The Day God Played With Me!

By T.C. Bryant

The true story of a little boy, his kite and his encounter with God

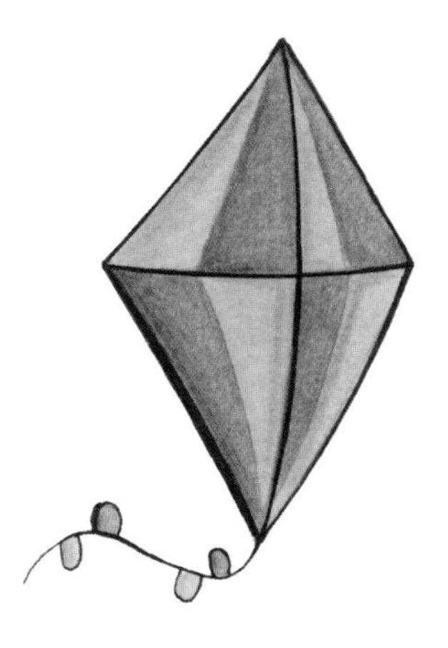

The Day God Played With Me!
by T.C. Bryant

Illustrations by Erik Lopez

Printed in the United States of America

ISBN 9781625091291

A 

Production
http://www.glorymakers.com/

www.xulonpress.com

Dedication

As a writer, I want to recognize the people who believed in me and have helped to make this book for young people possible. I dedicate this book to my wife, Irene, my son, Steve and grandchildren, Keekee, Deedee, Dakota and Dash Cornell.

Intro

I was thrilled as I sensed the Spirit of God stirring my heart to do this project. Spiritually, it so complimented two of my greatest passions, discernment and obedience to God.

Today, in our upside down world it is important that we seriously practice and train ourselves to live as sensitive to the voice and leading of God as possible. More times than often, many of us allow our daily activities to interfere with what should be necessary in our day to day lives.

My prayer is that this true story, written for young people, would draw all ages to a more real and true relationship with their Savior. To some it may be the starting point and to others it may be the challenge to go spiritually deeper. To me this is the most relevant thing that can be done on any given day.

I am challenging parents, teachers, and caretakers to join me everyday by encouraging the reading of this amazing true story. We have also included some powerful character pointers for teaching and open discussion.

TOW
TOW

Lit'l T.C. grew up in the West End ghetto of Houston, Texas- known as the big 'H' town. Good role models were scarce for him. His special gift of visions and dreams kept him entertained for hours; yet he didn't know they were coming from God.

Character Pointer:

Keep a journal and write your dreams and visions down.

Chang's Groceries
OPEN
STOP
WE

Everyday, Lit'l T.C. and his neighborhood friends would meet at the corner grocery store to buy snacks and then go play ball in the middle of the street.

Character Pointer:

Choose good friends.

NEW

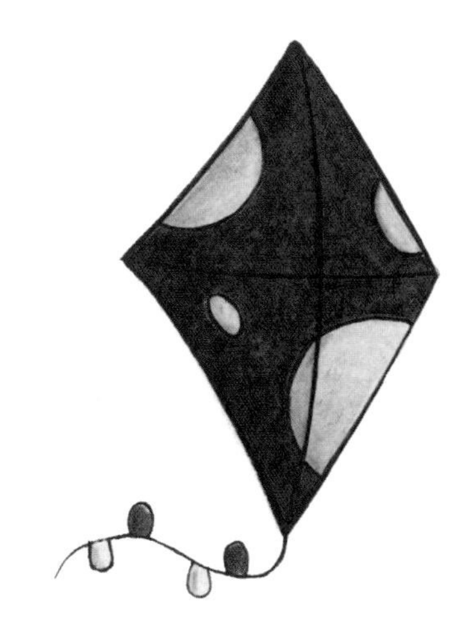

One day, Mr. Chang, the neighborhood store owner, shared a new display of colorful, diamond-shaped paper kites he had just brought into his store. He showed them how to put the kites together. It was the boys' first time learning about kites, and Lit'l T.C. and his friends got all excited about buying their first new kites!

Character Pointer:

Be adventurous by trying something new and different.

Since the streets were too dangerous and the empty lots were too weedy for flying their new kites, they discovered that they could use the new freeway while it was still under construction. The site had earthmovers, hanging generators, and long-neck cranes! On weekends, it became their imaginary park for climbing dirt hills, playing games and flying kites.

Character Pointer:

Always have faith and believe for better outcomes.

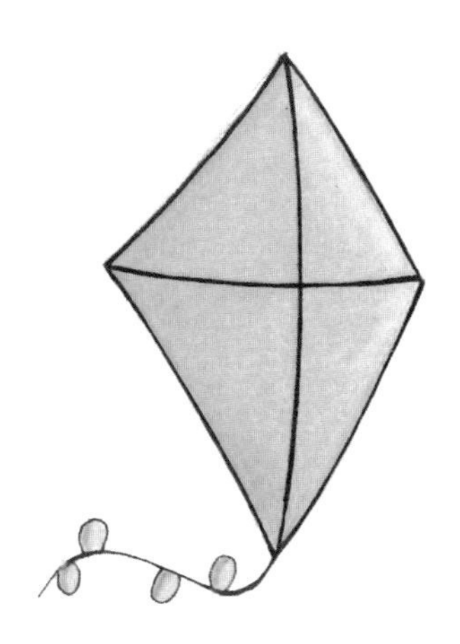

One day, they decided to fly their kites with Lit'l T.C.'s kite going up first. Suddenly, his kite started rising quickly, going higher and higher. He had to send his friends to the store to keep buying more spools of string! But still Lit'l T.C.'s kite kept going higher than any he had ever heard or seen. Again, he sent his friends to buy more spools of string but it still kept going unbelievably higher!

"WOW!" was all he could hear from his friends as they cheered with joy and excitement.

Character Pointer:

Negative situations can be turned into wonderful opportunities.

For a long time Lit'l T.C. tried very hard to bring his kite back. As he pulled back on the string, it continued to go even higher! It felt like someone was tugging on his kite, playing with him from the clouds. He stood there staring into the blue sky that was darkening moment by moment, his kite soaring higher and higher. He tried one last time but to no avail. So he prayed asking God to bring his kite down.

Character Pointer:

There are times mysteries may go unknown and yes many times during the pursuit of life their significance becomes clear.

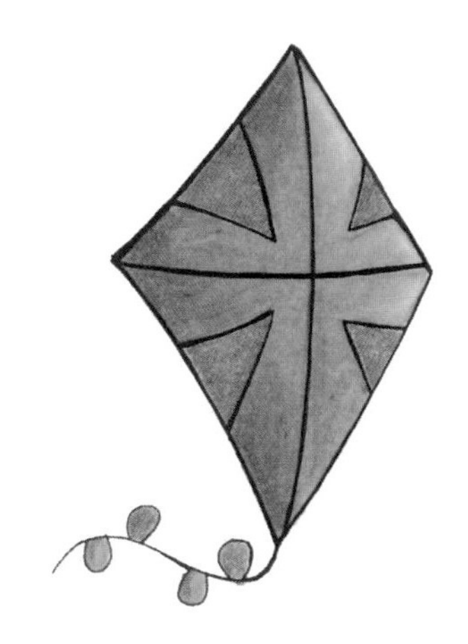

Lit'l T.C. held on to the kite string as he stared into the sky. His friends realized it was impossible to recover and they started saying to him, "You're losing it! You're losing it!" He struggled - it was too hard for him to let go of. So the fight for his kite continued.

Character Pointer:

Never give up.

The sun was setting, and daylight was quickly fading; Lit'l T.C.'s friends started to leave. In his heart, he knew he had to let go and give up on the kite, so he finally released it. He watched it go into the heavens. At first he was sad, but then a beautiful thought came to him. God has it! Then he said out loud, "God has my kite!" That's when Lit'l T.C. realized GOD HAD PLAYED WITH HIM!

Character Pointer:

Remain positive and hopeful in all situations.

H
ON
WON

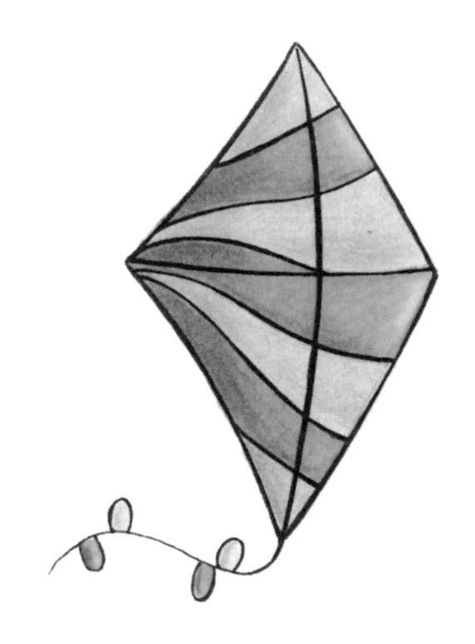

Lit'l T.C. has never forgotten his unforgettable kite or that day. It was the talk among all his friends. That day, he believed that God was real. He grew closer to God as he discovered that God was involved with the playing and fun parts of his life. With joy and gladness in his heart his face beamed with excitement about God, his new friend and playmate.

Character Pointer:

Appreciate the moments of your life;
you only live once, (Yolo).

Erik was raised in Delicias, Chihuahua, Mexico. At the age of twelve, he immigrated to El Paso, Texas, with his family, each one determined to acquire a better education and standard of living.

Art has always played a key role in his life. His passion towards drawing and designing led him to pursue a Bachelor's of Arts degree in graphic design at the University of Texas at El Paso. Erik believes that with passion, commitment, and faith in God, he will see bigger and greater accomplishments reached. This book is Erik's first illustration.

Erik Lopez

CPSIA information can be obtained
at www.ICGtesting.com
Printed in the USA
LVXC02n1917050814
397706LV00002B/3